GIG CATHARSIS

Alice Wickenden is a precarious academic and writer from Essex. She specialises in early modern literature and the history of libraries and writes prose as well as poetry. In her spare time, she volunteers for Abortion Support Network.

Also by Alice Wickenden

how to decode your orange-peel fortunes   (Nine Pens Press, 2022)

To Fall Fable   (Variant Literature, 2021)

Thriftwood   (Broken Sleep Books, 2021)

CONTENTS

CARPE DIEM POEM IN THE FACE OF A CLIMATE CRISIS	9
CLOSE READING OF AN APOLOGY STATEMENT	17
ACKNOWLEDGEMENTS	25

© 2024, Alice Wickenden. All rights reserved; no part of this book may be reproduced by any means without the publisher's permission.

ISBN: 978-1-916938-41-0

The author has asserted their right to be identified as the author of this Work in accordance with the Copyright, Designs and Patents Act 1988

Cover designed by Aaron Kent

Edited and Typeset by Aaron Kent

Broken Sleep Books Ltd
PO BOX 102
Llandysul
SA44 9BG

Gig Catharsis

Alice Wickenden

Broken Sleep Books

how do you reconcile the truth
of that with the truth of this?

CARPE DIEM POEM IN THE FACE OF A CLIMATE CRISIS

i.
Had we but world enough and time,
I would write a poem scented bitter like these days:
coffee, lemon, ferment.
The way we feed each other. I would
tell you about how I walked home
weighed down with ripe fruit and cans
that jangled like some rag-and-bone man's call,
that looked forward to their own recycling

All you would have to do is take what I offered
and give back what you could
put on
clothes someone else bought
dress your beautiful body.
And for a moment we would be unaware that we cruise
six miles above the sea-for-sale, that
we tumble towards the end of the world
and are to blame. How many trees died
for this poem?

Once, exhausted by the spectre of late capitalism
and the London grey, you spent fifteen quid to fly to Germany
and see the woman you almost married. She is tanned
happier
than you. Was it worth it?
A weekend of bolstering up your crumbling spirit
in exchange for everything?

Soon we will have no food at all
we will have nothing
but the sun...

Hasn't that always been the aim? Won't the lovers rejoice?
Nothing but flame-licked skin and metaphors for death
as far as the eye can see? Can you feel them licking
at your back? Not time's chariot but death's.

When does the skeleton *stop* being a metaphor?

(When it's yours)
Let us cling together and fuck without desire of procreation
Had we but world enough and time I would tell you that there is
nothing anyway
I would say

carve out a moment with me in lieu of a future

ii.
The ugly truth of the matter is
stuck in your throat
spit me out sharp

as a thankless child
(*King Lear* – a man

raging against his dead wife,
his girls who refuse to offer him

silence, which in women
is equivalent to love, and

when they grow thorns
he chokes)

bitter blistered seed
from fruit you don't

even remember
eating   but

that's how it gets you
it's in the air

chemtrails
you know

*

mythology is not kind to children
or animals
it's like film in that sense

*

this is not the retelling of a story you already know
this is far, far less
this is B-grade podcast shit
this is the truth twenty times removed from itself,
$$\text{if you look closely}$$

*

I want to die
& be reborn a dying sun

I have a friend who in her past life was a beetle

when you ask what species she says *it's extinct now*
and humans never knew it existed
maybe I was the last of my kind

I think she's bullshitting
but then again

*

fairytales are so cruel, right?

                        the world is burning

the evil stepmother

                        the world is *burning*

the useless father

                        I don't think I will live to 80

the brilliant daughter

                        I tell my parents this and they
                        hope I am joking

    denial / denial / denial / denial / denial / denial / denial / denial

                        I didn't mean to write a climate change poem
                        but my best friend is pregnant &
                        I am happy for her &
                        I am terrified

*

maybe we are at the beginning of the myth

the mulch from which something beautiful will spring
maybe this is the part of the story where all hope is lost

*

Mother Earth?
thankless fucking children.
sorry I don't have anything better to offer

I think we are out of time –

[exeunt]

iii.

Did you know?
The concept of a carbon footprint was created by BP.
Obscene oil slurping, shitting out
oligarchs rinsing *our* yoghurt pots, recycled in batches of
(30 people on our burning planet speak Klingon fluently)

In the airplane I am seated next to the Corpus of Dead Languages
We share crisps. I don't understand a word she says
(I can't even begin to transliterate)

bangwi' soh I say, which is Klingon for *my beloved one*
(in case she is asking why I am deigning to destroy our home)
(I love you too much and Earth will die because of it)

iv.
how do you reconcile the truth
of that with the truth of this?

CLOSE READING OF AN APOLOGY STATEMENT

"I saw you last night drinking

tap-cold water
straight from the source

splattering your perfect
roll-neck jumper

soaking the faded band t-shirt hidden underneath. That album

meant the most to you,
more than any other ever did,

but the lead singer – well –
you know.

You can't bring yourself to
throw it away

or to be seen having
his name next to your soft skin.

But still the music hangs in your heartbeat...

//

and the night you saw it live

you screamed / catharsis
amongst the crowd / cried into
your five-quid can / of red stripe /

lipstick smudged / but who cares in the dark? /

And you danced.

I saw you dance /

god it is good to dance.

I thought you had forgotten

how to move.

When the allegations came out
you said nothing

but I know it's there.
I see the way you want to
dance."

//

"I was in the crowd

waiting for the support band

when a whisper ran through the room (like a river)

everyone went to piss / buy a pint / browse the merch / check their phones /

(which is how
the rumour came)

I turned to the girl next to me
(she'd come from Sweden)

& her eyes wide (as apples) she said softly

(fuck)

//

but the night I saw it live

I peered hoarse through crowds of bodies in the same sticky space choking and crying as if they'd never been alive before and never would be again, which for all I know they never would be, and certainly my heart has never beaten since, and the lead singer held his hand out to us, and we yearned for it like disciples, like his touch could save us, like his words could absolve us:

I just wanted to talk about depression… because things aren't always easy, sometimes you struggle to get out of bed, I know, if things are hard for you right now… they're hard for me too… and it's not your fault, I just want you to know it's not your fault…

and how bittersweet the realisation that our faith was misspent, that just because we thought he recognised our sadness does not mean we were safe, but yes to answer your question, sometimes it comes on shuffle and before my brain has come online my body starts to move and grieve communal, my heart starts beating again, yes for a moment music does whatever it is that it does, which I surely cannot be blamed for, feminist morals aside, it happens beyond the brain, music, music, and so yes to answer your question my blood recognises it and my blood loves it and I think no matter what he did it always will, it is inside me the way we moved as a crowd, snake-like, seductive, screaming together
and I can see you disagree but I don't know what to say, I wish I had never heard it, but it's beyond my control, and that song is in me now, isn't it? and that's what happens when an album saves your life? if you cut me open it would still be there and that's no-one's fault, that's just what music does, isn't it? that's just love, just blood?

//

isn't it?"

//

(I don't have an answer
but *god*, it is good to dance)

//

how do you reconcile the truth
of that

with the truth of this?

ACKNOWLEDGEMENTS

Part III of '*Carpe Diem*' was originally drafted in conversation with Harry Man following an invitation from S.J. Fowler to create something for the European Poetry Festival 2022; it would not exist without them.

LAY OUT YOUR UNREST

Milton Keynes UK
Ingram Content Group UK Ltd.
UKHW030003260824
447288UK00004B/157